# Namibia:
# A General Introduction

## Willie Seth

Namibia: A General Introduction

First Edition

ISBN 9781081136949

New Africa Press

# Introduction

THIS is a very simple introduction to the country of Namibia, one of the continent's most fascinating.

It is not an in-depth study of the country. It only provides some basic facts about one of Africa's largest countries in terms of area.

The book may help members of the general public and tourists to get a general picture of Namibia without being boggled in details which can be obtained elsewhere by those who are interested in learning more about the country.

It is therefore not intended for serious students or subject specialists who are doing scholarly research on Namibia.

If you are interested in learning just a few facts about Namibia in order to get a comprehensive picture of this great land and its people only in general terms, you may find the book to be helpful. It may even encourage you to learn more about the country and the people who inhabit this magnificent land.

# General Background

NAMIBIA is one of the largest countries in Africa – fifteenth-largest. It is also the thirty-fourth largest in the world. But it is also one of the least populated. It has only about 2.6 million people in an area of more than 318,000 square miles.

A large part of the country is occupied by the Namib desert from which the country gets its name. The desert is mostly along the coast although, in some parts, it is more than 100 miles wide.

Namibia is bordered by the Atlantic Ocean on the west, South Africa in the south and southeast, Botswana in the east, Zambia in the northeast, and by Angola in the north.

It is also very close to Zimbabwe, separated by only 220 feet. The two countries don't share a border.

It is the driest country in Africa south of the Sahara and has the least amount of rainfall. But it has fertile areas especially in the north.

The majority of the people belong to the Ovambo ethnic group who migrated from the Great lakes region of East Africa in the 1500s and overpowered the indigenous people – the San, Damara and Nama – in the area that came to be known as the Germany colony of South West Africa, now independent Namibia.

Although a large part of Namibia is desert, it is one of the most prosperous countries on the continent with a major mining industry. Agriculture, livestock and tourism are also major sectors of the economy together with mining and manufacturing. And had it not been for the Namib desert, the country would have more people than it does now.

Only 4,000 white commercial farmers own 50 per cent of the arable land. Together with other whites, they control about 90 per cent of Namibia's land.

White farmers do play a major role in the economic life of the nation. But disparity in land ownership is one of the contentious issues that has not been resolved and threatens the country's future and stability if it is not addressed. As Mabasa Sasa stated in "Namibia: Landless In The Land Of The Brave" in the *New African*, 15 February 2013:

"At the close of Namibia's ruling party, SWAPO's fifth congress on 2 December 2012, party leader and state president Hifikepunye Pohamba disclosed that a raft of major issues had been highlighted during deliberations and these would be dealt with expeditiously. Among them were 'accelerated land reform and land redistribution" and "addressing the access and affordability of residential land in urban and peri-urban areas.'

A few statistics will put the criticality of the land issue into perspective: White Namibians make up about 6% of Namibia's population of 2.4 million people, other non-black groups (mostly mixed race) make up less than 8%, and the rest (about 76%) are black Africans.

But whites control nearly 90% of the land in what is the world's 34th largest country by area. And around 50% of the arable land is in the hands of just about 4,000 white commercial farmers.

In this country of skewed land ownership, experts say the GDP per capita in 2005 was $2,334 (Africa's average was $681), but the richest 5% of the population – mostly whites – take about 71%. At the same time, the poorest 55% account for 3% of GDP.

This has seen Namibia characterised as one of the most unequal societies on Earth, something that is rarely mentioned in the media. The whites who enjoy all this wealth are mostly descendants of German and South African colonisers, and many of them are absentee landowners who live permanently in South Africa, Italy, Germany and other places.

According to Dr Wolfgang Werner, who soon after Namibia's independence in 1990 served as director of lands in the Ministry of Lands, Resettlement and Rehabilitation:

'The racially-weighted distribution of land was an essential feature in the colonial exploitation of Namibia's resources, directly affecting the profitability not only of settler agriculture, but also of mining and the industrial sector.

As in pre-independence Zimbabwe, the whole wage structure and labour supply system depended critically on the land divisions in the country. Access to land determined the supply and cost of African labour to the colonial economy. So, large-scale dispossession of black Namibians was as much intended to provide white settlers with land, as it was to deny black Namibians access to the same land, thereby denying them access to commercial agricultural production and forcing them into wage labour.'

It is against this background that at its December party congress, President Pohamba and SWAPO included the land issue amongst the most pressing in Namibia. But how is it that this situation prevails 23 years after independence?

When apartheid South Africa finally succumbed to local military and international diplomatic pressure in 1990 and left Namibia, the new government tried to institute a process of land reform.

However, as in all independence pacts, crucial clauses were inserted in the constitution to ensure that "private property" remained protected and the status quo was preserved.

In Namibia's case, this was Article 16(2) of Chapter 3 of the constitution, which says:

'The state or a competent body or organ authorised by law may expropriate property in the public interest subject to the payment of just compensation, in accordance with requirements and procedures to be determined by [an] Act of Parliament.'

More broadly, this is interpreted as the "willing-buyer, willing-seller" system, in which the state cannot acquire land for redistribution unless the landholder actually wants to let go of it. Crucially, the seller has to agree to the price offered by the government.

This condition, it is widely accepted, came about as a result of the efforts of the "Contact Group", which comprised the UK, USA, Canada, Germany and France, as a means of ensuring SWAPO could not deliver on its key liberation grievance of large-scale land redistribution.

As such, between 1990 and 2002, only 1% of commercial land changed hands from whites to blacks, and by the mid-1990s less than 20 freehold farms had been purchased for redistribution.

Available figures indicate that as at November 2011, the government had bought 293 farms covering some 1.8 million hectares at about $66m. This translated to 4,790 families resettled against a waiting-list of nearly 200,000.

Namibia's First National Development Plan (1995-2000) committed $2.4m per year for purchasing commercial farms, and a similar figure was set aside for the same purposes under the Second National Development Plan (2001-2005).

The annual budget for land acquisition was increased to $5.9m in 2003, and there are indications that this could soon be doubled. Even then, going by what was paid for

293 farms in the first 12 years of independence, the figure could turn out to be woefully inadequate as land prices rise.

The government says it aims to acquire 15.3 million hectares of land by 2020; 5 million for direct resettlement and the rest through an Affirmative Action Loan Scheme. With the current pace of redistribution, such a target remains unlikely – unless radical reforms are instituted.

The government has responded to the land pressure by coming up with new regulations that it hopes will speed up the process of acquisition. However, it remains a willing-buyer, willing-seller system. In essence, the new model allows commercial farmers to tell the government they are not interested in selling land in a shorter space of time.

According to a Lands and Resettlement Ministry newsletter, farmers can now withdraw their offer of selling land to the state if they do not like the initial offer price or how negotiations are proceeding. The government then moves on to the next farmer. 'This model opens the way for flexibility and negotiations between government and the landowner before the ministry makes a final counter-offer,' the Lands Ministry says. Previously, once a farmer made an offer of sale to the state, s/he could not withdraw it and the two parties would be locked in never-ending negotiations with the Lands Tribunal standing available for price determination.

'The [new] mechanism has been rigorously tested since then and has proved to be doable and beneficial to all parties,' the Lands Ministry insists.

This means farmers can easily price the land out of the government's reach much quicker than previously, something that Namibia's founding president, Dr Sam Nujoma, fumed about in an interview with the regional weekly paper, *The Southern Times*: 'We thought that when we have adopted the policy of national reconciliation, those whites who remained with us in Namibia, [would] also accept our policy of land reform, but we see now they are sabotaging land reform,' said a furious Dr Nujoma.

Land reform remains premised on the National Resettlement Policy and Resettlement Criteria, which are thankfully now under review.

The criteria stems from the 1991 National Land Reform conference, which adopted 24 'consensus resolutions' that inform the laws and policies governing tenure changes. Apart from the willing-buyer, willing-seller system, there can be no claims on the grounds of 'ancestral land' and priority is on expropriating farms from absentee landlords. Amendments through a proposed Land Bill, to peg maximum farm sizes in communal areas to 20 hectares and to identify under-utilised land among other measures, could also mean more people getting access to land. But the question is: why are the farm sizes of the already disadvantaged being limited in a country where it is not unusual for a white farmer to own 20,000 or more hectares of land?

## Zero cases in 20 years!

There are several legal and political routes that the state can pursue to meet its obligations to the land hungry, one of which is using the Lands Tribunal more effectively. The Tribunal was established to act as an arbiter in disputes between the willing-buyer and the willing-seller.

According to the Ministry of Lands and Resettlement:

'The Lands Tribunal is mainly tasked with the determination of the purchase price of farms in the event where the farm owner concerned [does] not agree [with] the counter-offer made by the minister in respect of the farm offered and the owner makes an application to the Lands Tribunal.'

The Ministry's website gives the Lands Tribunal's jurisdiction as:

*Deciding any appeal lodged with it in terms of any provision of the Act.

*Considering and giving a decision on any application made to it in terms of any provision of the Act.

*Generally inquiring and adjudicating upon any matter which is required or permitted to be referred to it under any provision of this Act or any other law.

The Tribunal has as much authority as the High Court of Namibia, and thus carries sufficient weight to ease things along. But according to the chair of the Tribunal, Advocate Dirk Conradie, the institution is yet to hear a single case. That's right, zero cases in 20 years!

In an interview with *New African (see pages 42-43)*, Conradie could barely hide his frustration, both as a Namibian and as a professional, at the under-use of the Lands Tribunal. In his view, the state is yet to exhaust the options available to it.

'The government can simply state maximum farm sizes and start reallocating the 'excess' land,' he says. 'There is no justice in one person having 70,000 hectares of land – which was illegally seized from indigenous populations during colonialism – when hundreds of thousands of people have nothing.

'After that, the state must go after absentee landlords. This has been done to some extent but the mechanisms must be tightened. Why should a person own 20,000 hectares that they use as a holiday resort for two months of the year and then spend the other 10 months in Germany or wherever else?'

Conradie adds that a major area that needs revisiting to unlock land access is that of 'illegally obtained land'. According to him: 'Any transfer of land requires a waiver from the Ministry of Lands and Resettlement, even if that land is owned by a closed corporation. But what we have are white lawyers in this country facilitating the transfer of land from one closed corporation to another without seeking clearance from the state.

'The Ministry of Trade should avail a register of the properties of closed corporations, so that if they own land no asset transfers can be done without the Ministry of Lands being aware.'

What he means is this: a private company that owns farmland can sell out to another private company, and ownership of that land is thus transferred without the government being aware of it.

Since no waiver has been granted for the transfer of that land, the land is 'illegally obtained' and should thus be automatically forfeited to the state.

Conradie thinks 'the government should conduct an audit on which companies own what land and how they acquired it.'

Another major handicap in the present system is that of the jurisdiction of the Lands Tribunal. While it enjoys the same status as the High Court, it also appears to share jurisdiction with that institution.

This means an aggrieved party can opt to take a land dispute to the High Court rather than the Lands Tribunal, and that is more likely to happen as Conradie's views on land reform are well known. As long as white farmers can get recourse to the High Court, they will not go to the Lands Tribunal. President Pohamba knows that Namibia is sitting on a timebomb.

In an interview with *Al Jazeera* last year, the president said: 'Inequality exists… people are not happy, and when you talk about people not being happy, what do you expect? They can react. And when they react, then those who have the land will not have the land, people will take over the land.'

Political and legal options are there for Namibia, but will they be taken? The late Prof Archie Mafeje of the University of Cape Town (South Africa) once cast aspersions on the political will of Namibia's rulers and the wealthy.

'The whole debate about land in Namibia is not about the livelihood of the dispossessed in the countryside but about how best to maintain the status quo,' he said. 'This could be true of white farmers, the government, as well as the black notables in the so-called communal areas.'
But how long can this situation continue?"

# The people of Namibia

A vast country, Namibia is also sparsely populated. It is the least densely populated country in the world besides Mongolia which has the lowest population density among all countries.

Much of the country is occupied by the Namib and Kalahari deserts.

Namibia does not get much rain. The arid nature of the country has had a direct impact on the economy and the people's wellbeing.

It is very hard to grow crops in such a climate. Livestock is the pillar of the agricultural sector, with cattle being dominant in the northern part of the country, and sheep and goats in the south.

About 60 per cent of Namibians live in the more fertile northern part of the country. The southern and coastal areas have very people.

At least 50 per cent of the people depend on agriculture as a means of livelihood – food and income. The main products from agricluture are dairy goods, and harvest crops such as millet, sorghum, groundnuts and grapes.

Although the country is sparsely populated, it has a high unemployment rate. One of the factors contributing to high unemployment is lack of land ownership which in most countries across the continent – and in other parts of the Third World – is a form of life insurance. Most black Namibians don't have arable land because it is in the hands of only a handful of whites, a colonial legacy that has yet to be fully addressed.

Namibia, like South Africa, is known for its minerals. The country has a developed mining industry. Diamonds are the main export. Other major minerals for export include lead, silver, copper, tin, zinc, uranium, and tungsten. The country also has large deposits of iron and natural gas which have note yet been fully exploited.

Another major economic activity is fishing. The country also has an important but small manufacturing sector producing mainly processed foods.

Besides minerals, other export products include cattle, Karakul pelts, fish. Neighbouring South Africa is Namibia's main trading partner.

One ethnic group, the Ovammbo, is dominant in the country. Almost 50 per cent of the Namibia's population is composed of the members of this ethnic group. They live mostly in the northern part of the country. But they also live in other parts of the country, mainly in towns and other urban centres where they have settled in search of employment, education and the attraction of urban life and industrialisation.

Other major groups are the Kavango, the second-largest, although a distant second, constituting about 9 per cent of Namibia's population; Coloureds including Basters, 8 per cent; the Herero, the Damara, the Himba, and whites, each constituting 7 per cent of Namibia's population.

Others are the Nama, about 5 per cent of the population; the Lozi, also known as Caprivians, who make up about 3.5 per cent of the population. They live mostly in the Caprivi Strip in the northeastern part of the country and tried to secede after Namibia won independence from South Africa.

The San, also known as Bushmen, are 3 per cent of Namibia's population. The Tswana, 0.6 per cent, and other various groups together constitute the rest of the population of 0.5 per cent. They include refugees from Angola – and their descendants – who fled to Namibia during the wars in Angola, and a significant number of Chinese, about 40,000, of them in 2006.

White Namibians are mostly Afrikaner, German, British and Portuguese. Together, they constitute the second-largest number of whites in Africa – south of the Sahara – surpassed only by those in South Africa.

Most whites and Coloureds – as well as Basters – in Nambia speak Afrikaans. And a large number of them, about 30,000, are of German origin descended from the German settlers who ruled and controlled Namibia when the country was their colony before they lost it the British after being defeated in World War I. And almost all the Portuguese in Namibia came from Angola which was a Portuguese colony until 1975 when the country won independence.

Most of the people in Namibia are Christian. They constitute about 80 per cent of the population and are mostly Protestant. About 50 per cent of them are Lutheran. Followers of traditional religions constitute about 10 per cent of the population. And a significant number of black African Christians believe in the sanctity of traditional religious beliefs even when they clash with Christian teachings.

About 10,000 Namibians are Muslim, mainly members of the Nama ethnic group. And there are a few Jews, about 100 of them, but more in neighbouring South Africa with which Namibia has had strong historical, cultural and economic ties since its founding as a German colony.

English is Namibia's official language. Although Afrikaans and German were also official languages together with English when the country was ruled by apartheid South Africa, most Africans shunned those languages because of their connection to the colonial and racist rulers who ruled and oppressed them.

English is spoken mainly by urban residents, young people and northerners such as the Ovambo.

English is also being used to forge a new and strong

national identity that is not linked to or identified with the colonial languages – German and Afrikaans – which symbolised racial oppression. As Godfrey Mwakikagile states in his book, *Namibia: Conquest to Independence: Formation of a Nation*:

"The quest for unity in diversity has also entailed the adoption of a neutral language, English, as Namibia's official language. In the absence of an indigenous language that is accepted as the *lingua franca*, the government of Namibia felt that it had no other choice besides adopting English as the official language.

Although Oshivambo is spoken by about 50 per cent of the people of Namibia, it is an ethnic language clearly identified with the Ovambo ethnic group. Its adoption as the country's official language would have caused an uproar among non-Ovambos in the country and would never have been accepted as the national language unless all the other native languages were accorded the same status as happened in South Africa after the end of apartheid.

Namibia decided not to take that approach, giving all indigenous languages official status which would have amounted to what the government feared would be linguistic fragmentation of the country along ethnic lines (in a country that was already linguistically fragmented along those lines), and instead chose a language that was not identified with the white minority rulers, Afrikaners, in spite of the fact that Afrikaans is virtually Namibia's *lingua franca*.

Adoption of Afrikaans would have caused the same uproar it did in South Africa during the apartheid era when black students in Soweto refused to accept it as the medium of instruction and instead chose English, triggering the massacre of hundreds of black students by the security forces, an event that marked the beginning of the end of apartheid." – (Godfrey Mwakikagile, *Namibia: Conquest to Independence: Formation of a Nation*, Dar es Salaam, Tanzania: New Africa Press, 2015, pp. 161 – 162).

The language which has the largest number of speakers in Namibia is Oshiwambo (also written as Oshivambo) – or Oshiwambo dialects – spoken by members of the largest ethnic group in the country, the Ovambo. It is followed by Nama/Damara spoken by 11 per cent of Namibians who belong to those ethnic groups; Afrikaans by 10 per cent; Kavango and Herero, each by 9 per cent of Namibians.

About 60 per cent of white Namibians speak Afrikaans, 32 per cent of them speak Germans, 7 per cent English, and 1 per cent Portuguese.

Although English is Namibia's official language, Afrikaans is almost the country's lingua franca. It is spoken by most black Africans – who constitute the vast majority of Namibia's population – together with their tribal languages and English which is spoken a smaller number of them.

# Ovambo

The Ovambo not only constitute the vast majority of the people in northern Namibia; they are also native to Angola, across the border, where they are commonly as Ambo while in Namibia they are known as Ovambo. They are also a minority in Angola, constituting about 2 per cent of the country's population.

Although they are collectively identified as one people, which they are, the Ovambo are an amalgamation or collection of 12 sub-tribal groups. The largest is the Kwanyama constituting about 35 per cent of the Ovambo population, followed by the Ndonga and the Kwambi, respectively, with 30 per cent and 12 per cent.

Other Ovambo groups are the Mbalanhu, the Ngandyela, the Unda, and the Nkolonkadhi, listed here not necessarily in descending order of population size.

The traditional home of the Ovambo, known as Owamboland, is divided into four regions: Ohangwena, Omusati, Oshana and Oshikoto.

The main means of livelihood for the Ovambo is farming, growing millet and other crops; livestock and fishing – the region has many pools where the people catch fish.

In their traditional religion, the Ovambo believe in the existence of what they call Kalunga as the Supreme Being. But only about 3 per cent of them are followers of the traditional faith. The vast majority are Christian.

# Kavango

The people who live between the borders of Angola and Namibia are known as Kavango or the vaKavango. The is because the Kavango River in the northeastern part of Namibia forms a part of the border, an area which is also the heartland of the Kavango people. They are a collection of five groups: the Geiriku, the Mbunza, the Kwangari, the Mbukushu, and the Sambiyu.

The Kavango Region in the northeastern part of the country is their traditional homeland. They are closely related to the Ovambo and trace their origin to the Great Lakes region of East Africa and what is now Zambia. They migrated south to the area that became a part of Nambia in the 1500s.

The Kavango people are mainly farmers, growing maize, millet and sorghum. Fishing also is an important part of their lives; so is livestock, mainly cattle.

The people of Kavango Region also stand out in one respect: wood carving. They are excellent wood carvers. Most of the woo carvings found throughout Namibia come from Kavango.

They have strong kinship ties known as *ekoro*, equivalent to an extended family. Their traditional society is based on clans.

# Herero

Like the Ovambo and the Kavango, the Herero also migrated from the Great Lakes region of East Africa to what is now Namibia around the same time. They live mostly in central and eastern Namibia.

They are a collection of several sub-tribal groups including the Mahereo, Mbandero, Ndamuranda, Tjimba, and Zeraua.

They are also found in Botswana and Angola.

About 75 per cent of them were exterminated by the Germans during German colonial rule. Their estimated population during that time was 96,000. Only 16,000 survived. Some of the survivors fled to neighbouring Bechuanaland, now Botswana. It was the first genocide of the 20th century but is hardly acknowledged as such. As Godfrey Mwakikagile states:

"One of the saddest chapters in Namibia's and in Africa's history was the near-extermination of the Herero and the Nama, but mostly the Herero.

From 1904 to 1907, the Herero together with the Nama took up arms against their oppressors. The German colonial rulers responded with brute force.

Figures vary but up to 100,000 Hereros – about a third of the entire Herero population – were killed. And more than 10,000 Namas, who constituted half of the Nama population, lost their lives.

Tens of thousands of Hereros and a significant number of Namas were driven into the desert, without food and water, where they perished.

The extermination of the Herero and the Nama by the Germans is said to be the first genocide in the 20th century. The German government apologised to the people of Namibia in 2004 for this horrendous tragedy but refused to pay compensation for the atrocities." – (G. Mwakikagile, *Namibia: Conquest to Independence:*

*Formation of a Nation*, op. cit., p. 15).

The Herero are mostly pastoralists. Cattle are very important to them not only as source of wealth and means of livelihood but also for their cultural significance and symbolic value – demonstrated by their women's dresses which incorporate depictions of cow horns. Cattle ownership is as important to them as it is to the Maasai.

Their traditional belief is centred on Okuruo, which means holy fire. It is an intermediary between them and their ancestors who in turn speak to the Supreme Being on their behalf.

# Himba

The Himba, who are indigenous to Kunene Region in northern Namibia, are pastoralists. They move from one place to another in search of pasture for their livestock in their homeland, Kaokoland, in the northwest.

They are related to the Herero. They are descended from a group of Herero herders who settled in the northwestern part of Namibia after being pushed out of their traditional homeland by the Nama.

They are known for their traditional jewellery very popular with tourists.

# Damara

The Damara are a unique ethnic group in Namibia. They are Bantu. But their language is Khoisan. They speak the same language as the Nama but are not related to them. And they are probably the first Bantu group to migrate to the area that became Namibia.

The central part of the country was their land, a large area mostly inhabited by them, until they were forced out by the Nama and the Herero who moved in with their livestock in search of pasture.

That was not the end of their plight. The apartheid regime of South Africa which ruled Namibia – when it was known as South West Africa – forced the Damara to move out of their area and resettled them in a region called Damaraland which hardly had any rainfall or arable land.

After the end of white minority rule – and even before then but with more freedom thereafter – many of them moved into towns looking for jobs. Only a few of them, about 25 per cent of their total population, live in the area that was designated for them: Damaraland.

Traditionally the Damara own livestock, although not on a large scale, and grow crops including maize, pumpkins, tobacco and a variety of vegetables.

# Nama

The traditional homeland of the Nama was southern Namibia, around the Orange River, and northern part of South Africa. That was until the mid-1800s when they migrated to the area of what is Windhoek today.

They were called Hottentots – a disparaging term – when they lived in Namaqualand, their homeland, and even thereafter, and were forced to move north by European settlers who wanted their land.

Their forced migration north brought them into conflict with the Herero who had already occupied the area. The result was devastating.

The two groups fought many wars. And the German rulers resettled members of both groups in reserves, implementing a policy of apartheid decades before it came to be officially known as apartheid in the land of apartheid itself, South Africa, and practised in its colony of South West Africa acquired after Germany lost World War I.

The Nama – a collection of 13 subgroups – are linked to two groups in special ways. Their language has the same origin as the language of the Bushmen. They also speak

the same language the Damara do. They also have a light complexion like the Bushmen – the San – do.
They are some of the earliest practitioners of African socialism in terms of land ownership. Only one group among them, the Topnaars, does not have communal land.
One of Namibia's national heroes, Hendrik Witbooi, was a Nama. He is honoured as a leader in the struggle for independence because of the role he played in fighting German colonisers. His head is on Namibian bank notes to symbolise resistance of imperial rule and occupation.

# Topnaar

They are a branch of the Nama but distinct enough to be a group with its own identity.
Their homeland is along the Kuiseb River around Walvis Bay and have a unique history linked to a thorny desert plant, !nara melon. Their very existence and survival depended on this plant. It was an integral part of their diet and a source of income.
They were also hunters. But they are not allowed to hunt anymore because the areas where they used to hunt have been incorporated into the Namib-Naukluft park. Even their traditional source of food and income, !nara melon, faces virtual extinction because of water shortage in the area.

# Rehoboth Basters

They are descended from the Nama and and the Dutch and constitute one of the ethnic groups in Namibia. They are more than just a group of racially mixed people. They have also been known as Coloureds, besides Basters.
On their European ancestral side, they trace their origin to a group of Dutch families – a group of about 90 families – who migrated north to Namibia, from South Africa, and

finally settled in an area that came to be known as Rehoboth. When they arrived there, they found a group of the Nama, known as the Bondelswart, who had already occupied the area.

The Basters speak Afrikaans as their first language, which is also the "lingua franca" of Namibia.

The word "baster" means "bastard." But the Basters are not offended by the use of the term and are proud of their identity and history. They see themselves as different from other Coloureds because of their different origin, an identity reinforced by the fact that they have lived in the same area, Rehoboth – their homeland – for more than 100 years.

Although most of them still live in Reheboth, many of them have moved out in search of employment, especially in the nation's capital, Windhoek, where they work mostly in the building trade.

They are so proud of their unique identity that even after Namibia won independence, some of them wanted to have their own independent state and resorted to an armed "struggle" to achieve the goal. But it was only a few men who wanted to launch the liberation war even though many Basters may have shared the same "nationalist" sentiment.

# Coloureds

The Coloureds of Namibia trace their origin to the Cape Province of South Africa. They are related to the Basters, genetically, and speak the same language, Afrikaans. But their dialects and accents are different, giving the impression that they speak "different" languages – which only reinforces their separate identities even though coloured in both cases.

Most Coloureds live in Windhoek and Swakopmund and in other towns and villages where there are significant numbers of their people. They are also involved in fishing, especially in Walvis Bay, and in a wide range of activities in different fields including education, civil service and in various professions.

Like the Basters, the other racially mixed people, Coloureds had access to education more than blacks did because of racism. Black people were lowest in the racial hierarchy in terms of opportunities in all fields including manual labour where they also faced discrimination in wages and employment; whites still preferred employing racially mixed people.

# Caprivians

Caprivians, who are mostly farmers and fishermen, are divided into five groups: Lozi, Mbukushu, Subia, and Yei. Their homeland in the Caprivi Strip was once ruled by the Lozi.

# San

The San, or Bushmen, are the earliest inhabitants of the area that came to be the country of South West Africa, renamed Namibia. They also inhabited South Africa long before the arrival of Bantus from the north and before the coming of Europeans. Tragically, they were displaced – and mistreated – by both.

Even today, their wellbeing as hunters (they also, especially the women, gather plants for food) is threatened by the members of other groups around them – near and far – and by the impact of modernisation; a threat which, if it continues, could even lead to their extinction as a people. Expansion of commercial farming and mining are the biggest threats to their existence and wellbeing.

The Dutch settlers in South Africa, known as Boers, were even more ruthless. They exterminated about 200,000 of them in about two centuries and did not even consider them to be full human beings. Those who remain live mostly in the Kalahari Desert in Botswana; the remaining in Namibia and South Africa.

There are two areas in Namibia known for the preservation of creative art by the San: Twyfelfontein and the Brandberg. The art is believed to be thousands of years old.

# Tswana

The Tswana are one of the groups in Africa whose members are native to more than one country. They virtually constitute the nation of Botswana, after whom the country is named, where they are at least 80 per cent of the country's population.

They are also native to South Africa and Namibia. But their original homeland is northwest South Africa. In Namibia, they are the smallest ethnic group composed of three subgroups: Tlharo, Tlhaping and Kgalagadi. The Kgalagadi have intermingled – and intermarried – with the San of the Kalahari more than any other Namibian Tswana group.

The vast majority of the Tswana of Namibia live around Gobabis, a town in the eastern part of the country, not very far from the border with Botswana.

# Whites

Although most whites in Namibia speak Afrikaans, the German language and culture has left an imprint on Namibia totally out of proportion to the number of German settlers and their descendants who constitute a small minority of the white population. German colonisers ruled Namibia for only a few years. But their descendants have had impact virtually on all areas of life in Namibia's urban centres. Many businesses are owned by Namibians of German origin. Even the food in most Namibian restaurants and hotels in towns and cities is prepared the

German way.
Most whites in Namibia live in towns and cities, especially in Windhoek, Swakopmund, Walvis Bay and Tsumeb.

# Indigenes

Namibians who are considered to be indigenous to the area that came to be known as South West Africa, now Namibia, constitute only a small percentage of the country's total population even collectively – when they are counted together as one "group."

The San are the original inhabitants. Not all of them are hunters,as their ancestors have been for centuries – in fact for thousands of years. Many of them work on farms or grow their own crops and own livestock. They also work as domestic servants and are employed in other areas just like other Namibians especially in urban areas. They even own businesses.

Therefore, many of the have undergone fundamental changes in terms of life style through the years since the advent of colonial rule, first under Germany and next under apartheid South Africa.

They live mostly in central and northern Namibia. But they are also found in other parts of the country. And they are divided into three main groups: the Haillom who live in the Etosha area of north-central Namibia; the Khwe of Caprivi Region and Tsumkwe West; and the Jul'hoansi in Tsumkwe District East in the Otjozondjupa Region.

Tragically, more than 80 per cent of the San have lost their ancestral lands and resources, thanks to greed of other groups, especially whites, justified as "civilisation" and "modernisation" of "primitive" people and their areas. Because of all that, the San are some of the poorest and most marginalised people in Namibia and on the entire African continent. In fact, they live in worse conditions than all the other groups in Namibia.

Besides the San, the Himba are also acknowledged as an indigenous people of Namibia. The majority of them live in Kunene Region in the northwestern part of the country. They own livestock. They have close relations with the Herero who also own livestock and live in the central and eastern parts of Namibia.

The third ethnic group indigenous to the area that came to be known as Namibia is the Nama. The group includes the Topnaars. The Topnaars live in the Walvis Bay area and in the valley of the Kuiseb River. They own a few cattle and other livestock. The !nara melons are very important for their survival. They also earn a living from tourism.

One of the tragedies the indigenes face is that there are no special laws guaranteeing their rights as an endangered people. That is probably because the government says all Namibians have equal protection under the law, as indeed should be the case. But the prime minister's office did start programmes to help marginalised groups because of the extreme poverty they faced and still face more than other Namibians do.

# One people, one nation: National Identity

There is a strong sense of national identity among Namibians. The people are at the same time proud of their ethnic identities, sometimes at the expense of national harmony because of stereotypes about some groups by some people.

Yet there is no question that the country has made strides in buildidn and solidifying national unity by invoking the common identity all Namibians share as one people who belong to one nation. This is especially so among young peoplewho don't harbour stereotypes about other people the way older ones do.

Creation of a strong national identity has been facilitated by communication, interaction with other people from different parts of the country through employment and education, and migration to towns and other urban centres which serve as melting pots of different cultures when members from different ethnic groups meet, interact and live and work – as well as go to school – together.

Working in mines has also facilitated cultural and ethnic integration as members from different groups – almost all men – get the chance to know each other when they work and live together or in the same areas.

Unity in diversity has been one of the great achievements

of the people of Namibia in terms of nation building even though the country does not have many ethnic groups like most other African countries do; a point underscored by Godfrey Mwakikagile:

"Namibia does not have many ethnic groups or a large population as many other African countries do. But it has a number of groups which are profoundly different from each other; for example, the Baster, a product of mixed races; the Ovambo of Bantu stock; the San and the Khoikhoi, non-Bantu groups. Each group is unique its own ways.

It is this uniqueness of ethnic and cultural identity which has been one of the most effective tools in constructing a Namibian national identity in the post-apartheid era on the basis of unity in diversity when it can be a disruptive force if not carefully managed or if it is exploited by unscrupulous politicians for partisan interests and by other people in pursuit of whatever agenda they want to pursue at the expense of national unity." – (G. Mwakikagile, *Namibia: Conquest to Independence: Formation of a Nation*, op.cit., p. 161).

Yet in spite of Namibia's achievement in forging a single national identity, ethnic loyalties and even rivalries remain a major problem with significant potential for fracturing the country along ethno-regional lines if they are not contained and possibly neutralised.

Ethnic rivalries and loyalties – as well as regional interests – are a major factor in national politics where a delicate balance in terms of power is needed to appease and satisfy all groups and regions.

There have even been attempts by some groups to restore old glories – of traditional centres of power including kings – to solidify ethnic identities and justify claims to ancestral lands.

Even the official party, the Democratic Turnhalle Alliance (DTA), is a product of compromises among different ethnic organisations who agreed to form a political alliance as a counter-blance to the dominant ruling party,

SWAPO, dominated by the Ovambo.
De-facto segregation, especially in residential areas, persists, a legacy of apartheid when members of differences were separated and lived in their areas designated on racial basis to enforce the policy of racial separation which was sanctioned by law. Although this is no longer the law, the people themselves have been slow to change, with many of them preferring to live with their own kind on the basis of race and ethnicity. Economic barriers also impede integration even among those who would like to live with people of different races and ethnicities.

# Towns and cities

LIKE most African countries, Namibia is not highly urbanised. Therefore, it does not have very many towns and cities. However, its urban centres are more developed, relatively speaking, than those of other African countries except South Africa and a few others.

The terms "cities" and towns" also have their own unique or peculiar definition in the context of Namibia. They're distinguished by the status the Namibian government has given them. Urban centres with a municipality are known as cities; those with a town council are called towns.

**Windhoek**, the largest city in Namibia, is not only the nation's capital but its economic hub. It's also the nerve centre of Namibia in other fundamental respects in terms of social life, cosmopolitan outlook, international ties, and much more.

Windhoek is located in the central Khomas Region in a semi-desert area. It had a population of about 326,000 in 2011.

The city is the major commercial and financial centre of Namibia. The area where Windkoek is located was originally inhabited by the Herero.

Important landmarks in Windhoek include the Church of Christ, St. Mary's Cathedral, the Zoo Park, Tintenpalast, which in German means "Ink Palace," which is the seat of the Namibian legislature; and Alte Feste, German for "Old Fortress," which is home to the National Museum.

The University of Namibia, founded in 1992, is also

located in Windhoek. Other institutions of higher learning in Windhoek are Polytechnic of Namibia and the International University of Management.

**Walvis Bay** is second most well-known city or urban centre in Namibia.

Its name means "Whale Bay" in German. It's also the name of the bay on which the city is located.

The bay has been a haven for sea vessels because of its natural deepwater harbour.

Walvis Bay is the focal point for tourism in Namibia.

There are many government and private schools in Walvis Bay.

Fishing also is a major economic activity industry in Walvis Bay. The city also has wide open spaces, scenic beauty and unique marine and plant life.

The other cities in Namibia are Gobabis, Grootfontein, Hentiesbay, Karasburg, Karibib, Keetmanshoop, Mariental, Okahandja, Omaruru. Otavi, Otjiwarongo, Outjo, Swakopmund, Tsumeb, and Usakos.

**Gobabis** is the capital of the Omaheke Region in the eastern part of Namibia. The city is located in the heart of a cattle farming area.

Like many other towns in Namibia, Gobabis developed around a mission station. Gobabis means "place of discussion" in the Nama language. The town is in an area where the Herero and the Nama fought a number of wars.

And it continues to grow because of inter-territorial trade between Namibia and neighbouring Bostwana. A lot of export commodities and other goods from landlocked Botswana pass through Gobabis to the Namibian port of Walvis Bay. Also consumer goods from Johannesburg in South Africa imported by Namibia go through Gobabis.

The town had a population of 19,000 in 2011.

The most notable landmark that people see when entring the city is the Cattle Country Statue. It simply says, "Cattle Country."

**Grootfontein** is another city in Namibia. It had a population of about 24,000 in 2011 and is in Otjozondjupa Region. Its name means "Big Spring." There is a hot spring near the city.

But the largest city in Otjozondjupa Region is Otjiwarongo. It is also the regional capital and had a population of about 28,000 in 2011.

As in all towns in the Otavi triangle, Grootfontein is very green during summer which is from November to March. In spring, from September to November, it is blooming season for jacaranda and flamboyant trees.

The town is home to an old German fortress which serves as a museum for local history.

The largest meteorite in the world, the Hoba meteorite, is also located near Grootfontein. It weighs more than 60 tons and is also known to be the largest naturally occurring mass of iron known to exist on Earth.

**Henties Bay** is a coastal city in Erongo Region. It is mostly a holiday settlement.

**Karasburg** is the capital of the Karasburg Constituency. It is located in the heartland of the southern Namibian sheep farming industry. Its main economic activity is sheep farming. It is also an important stop for tracks and lorries going into Namibia from South Africa. And there are many large farms in the area.

The town also has the busiest train station in southern Namibia.

**Karibib** is a city and a constituency in Erongo Region in western Namibia. Its population was only about 4,000 in 2011. The headquarters of the Namibian Air Force is located north of this historic town – although it's called a city.

**Keetmanshoop** is a city in Karas Region in southern Namibia. It is named after Johann Keetman, a German industrialist and founder of the settlement.

Before the coming of Europeans, the area was known as Nu-gouses, meaning "Black Marsh" because of a spring in the area.

The Rhenish Mission Church in the town is a well-knwon

historic monument and a major tourist attraction. It is one of the architectural masterpieces – Gothic and African combined – in the country and a popular tourist attraction. The town is also an important commercial centre for the Karakul sheep farming community.

**Mariental** is a town in the south-central part of Namibia. It is located in a hot, arid region southeast of of the nation's capital Windhoek. It is a small market town and is the capital of Hardap Region, and area that for a long time has been home to members of the the the Nama ethnic group. It is near the Hardap Dam reservoir which is the largest lake in Namibia.

The dam has been developed as a popular watersport and holiday resort for tourists, campers, water-skiers and anglers. The dam is Namibia's first large earth-fill dam and supplies water to the area.

The town of Mariental is surrounded by commercial farms. They specialise in game farming, sheep, and cattle farming.

The Hardap Dam also provides irrigation for export crops such as graves and cotton, and alfalfa. The dam is also vital for dairy farming in the region.

**Okahandja** is a city in Otjozondjupa Region in the central part of Namibia. It was founded by the Herero and the Nama around 1800. The name of the city means "the place where two rivers flow into each other to form one wide one" in the Herero language.

There is an open-air curio market in town which is a major attraction for visitors and tourists. The town is also an administrative centre for the Herero who live in the area.

One of the nationalist leaders of Namibia, Clement Kapuuo, is buried in Okahandja. A school teacher and chief of the Herero, and a member of the founding committee of the nationalist party SWANU – the South West Africa National Union – he was a fierce opponent of colonial rule of his country by the apartheid regime of

South Africa and was assassinated in March 1978.

Also, the National Institute for Educational Development (NIED) has its headquarters in Okahandja. NIED was created after Namibia won independence.

The Von Bach Dam is also located near Okahandja. It provides most of the water for the nation's capital Windhoek.

The town is known for an annual festival during which the Herero remember their past local chiefs. It is also known for the dinosaur footprints which are located near Otjihenamaparero.

The town is also a historical site. The descendants of Lothar von Trotha and the von Trotha family went to Omaruru in October 2007 and publicly apologised for the role Lothar von Trotha played in the Herero genocide. He was the commander of the German forces which carried out the massacres. He played a similar role in German East Africa, now mainland Tanzania, where he ruthlessly suppressed anti-colonial uprisings including the famous uprising by the Hehe against German rule and brutal occupation of their land.

According to a BBC report, Wolf-Thilo von Trotha, publicly made this statement on behalf of the von Trotha family: "We, the von Trotha family, are deeply ashamed of the terrible events that took place 100 years ago. Human rights were grossly abused that time."

**Otavi** is an agricultural town in the mid-northern part of Namibia.

The towns of Otavi, Tsumeb and Grootfontein define area known as the OOtavi Triangle," also known as the Otavi Mountainland. This geographical region is also known as the "Golden Triangle" or as the "Mahangu Triangle" because of the cultivation of mahangu in the area. Mahangu is pearl millet and the main food for about half of Namibia's population.

The three towns which form this triangle are about 37 miles from each other. The area was once known for its minerals, now depleted.

The town's economy is dominated by two grocery stores, a

mill, two banks, two gas stations, game/cattle farms around the area and a few other small business. Most of them are owned by Afrikaners and Germans.

**Otjiwarongo** is located in Otjozondjupa Region in central north Namibia and also borders Botswana. It borders more regions that any other region in the country. Some of Namibia's best-known private game farms and nature reserves are located in and around Otjiwarongo.

The Herero first occupied the area and called it Otjiwarongo, meaning " The Place Where Fat Cattle Graze." The town's name is appropriate since some of the biggest cattle-breeding companies in the whole country are located there.

The town is near the Waterberg Plateau Park which draws many tourists.

The area is also is home to 20 per cent of the world's cheetahs, mostly on private ranch land.

About 90 per cent of the people in town speak or understand Afrikaans; 75 percent, English; and 35 per cent German. Native languages spoken in town include Herero, known as Otjiherero; Damara-Nama and Oshiwambo.

**Outjo** is a city in Outjo Constituency. It is best known as a gateway to Etosha National Park.

The town is near Gamkarab cave which is known fot its stalactites, stalagmites, and pietersite.

**Swakopmund** is a city on the Atlantic coast in the northwestern part of Namibia and 175 miles west of the nation's capital Windhoek. It is the capital of Erongo District and a famous seaside resort with a population of about 45,000 in 2011.

It was founded in 1892 as the main harbour of the colony of German South-West Africa and is famous for its German architecture.

Its attractions include Swakopmund Museum, the National Marine Aquarium, a crystal gallery and spectacular sand dunes.

Just outside the city is the Rossmund Desert Golf Course which is one of only 5 all-grass desert golf courses in the world.

There is a camel farm near the city, also the *Martin Luther* steam locomotive dating from 1896; it is lying in the desert.

Most of the urban centres in Namibia have their origin in native settlements. These settlements were mostly near sources of water. The native founders of those places named them in their native languages and when whites came, the new European settlers retained the original names but simplified them in order to make it easy to pronounce them; a practice that was common in many other parts of Africa where whites also settled. The names usually described the places where the native founders had settled.

When uranium was discovered near Swakopmund, the site of this important mineral became the largest opencast uranium mine in the world. The discovery had a big impact on Swakopmund, leading to the development and expansion of facilities in this urban centre making it one of the most developed in the entire country.

**Tsumeb** is a city in Oshikoto Region in the northern part of Namibia; it is also the largest in the region. It is sometimes referred to as the "gateway to the north." and is the closest town to the Etosha National Park. It had a population of about 20,000 in 2011.

Tsumeb was founded in 1905 by the German colonial rulers and became mostly a mining town.

There are two large sinkhole lakes near the town. And east of Tsumeb is one of the world's largest and deepest underground lakes on a farm known as Harasib.

The world's largest meteorite, a nickel-iron "heavenly" body estimated to weigh more than 60 tonnes and named Hoba or Hoba West, is located about forty minutes' drive east of Tsumeb. It is mostly iron, with smaller amounts of nickel and only traces of cobalt. It is classified as a national monument and attracts thousands of visitors every year.

**Usakos** is a city located 87 miles northeast of Swakopmund in Erongo Region. It is surrounded by mountains.

Arandis, known as the uranium capital of the world, is a town also in Erongo Region. The world's largest open-pit uranium mine, the Rössing Uranium Mine, is located just 9 miles outside Arandis. Most of the people who live in the town are somehow connected to the mine. The town had a population of about 5,000 in 2011.

**Eenhana** is a town in Ohangwena Region in the northern part of the country bordering Angola. It is also the regional capital and the largest town in the region.

The people from the other side of the border in Angola also cross into Namibia to shop in Eenhana. The also has a military base and a hospital among other facilities including the Oshinanena supermarket and a radio station and three-star hotels. It had a population of about 5,500 in 2011.

**Katima Mulilo** is a town in Caprivi Strip in northeastern Namibia. It is located on the Zambezi River in an area of lush riverine vegetation.

In mid-1999, there was an uprising in Caprivi Strip and demands for a separate independent state for the region.

The town is very close to the Namibia/Zambia border.

**Khorixas** is a town in Kunene Region in the southern part of Namibia. It once served as was the capital of Damaraland, a Bantustan established by the apartheid regime which ruled South West Africa before the country was officially renamed Namibia.

The capital of Kunene Region is a smaller and remote town known as Opuwo.

The region is mostly inhabited by members of the Damara ethnic group.

**Lüderitz** is a small town in the southwestern part of Namibia. It is a port known for Robert Harbour and for Shark Island. The town is located in one of the least hospitable coastal areas in Africa.

But the harbour is shallow and cannot handle modern ships; a disadvantage which led to the development of Walvis Bay as the centre of the shipping industry in the country. However, larger fishing vessels are able to use Robert Harbour because of the addition of a new quay.

The town had a population of about 12,500 in 2011.

Located just outside Lüderitz is the ghost town of Kolmanskop. It used to be a bustling diamond town.

South of Lüderitz, about 18 miles, is another ghost town, Elizabeth Bay.

**Nkurenkuru** is a town in Kavango Region. It is located on the south-western banks of the Okavango River. It was, until 1936, the capital for the entire region before the capital was moved to Rundu. Nkurenkuru is also home to the local Uukwangali kings. It is the second-largest and most important town in Kavango Region after Rundu.

**Okakarara** is a town and constituency in Otjozondjupa Region in north-central Namibia. The largest town in the region is Otjiwarongo which had a population of about 28,000 in 2011 while Okakarara had about 4,700 in the same year.

Okakarara is located about 31 miles southeast of Waterberg Plateau Park. The park is also 42 miles southeast of Otjiwarongo.

The area was a part of the Bantustan of Hereroland, created by the apartheid regime of South Africa, and is still mostly inhabited by the Herero.

**Ondangwa** is a town in Oshana Region in northern Namibia. Oshana borders Oshikoto Region. The town had a population of about 23,000 in 2011.

Most of the people in the town are Oshindonga and speak Oshindonga which is spoken in parts of Angola. It is a standardised dialect of the Ovambo language and is mutually intelligible with Kwanyama, another Ovambo dialect.

It is also a gateway to Etosha National Park.

**Ongwediva** is a town in Oshana Region in northern Namibia. It is the smallest region in the country. But the

Oshakati-Ongwediva-Ondangwa area has the second-largest population concentration in Namibia after the nation's capital Windhoek.

The town of **Oshakati**, which had a population of about 37,000 in 2011, is the capital of Oshana Region. It is the fourth-largest urban centre in Namibia and the largest in the northern part of the country. It is considered to be the capital of Ovamboland.

**Ongwediva** is also a town in Oshana Region and had a population of 27,000 in 2011. And most businesses in northern Namibia are located in Oshana Region.

Most of the people in Ongwediva speak Oshiwambo.

The town is also home to the University of Namibia's Faculty of Engineering and Information Technology. There is also an Educational College for training teachers.

**Opuwo** is the capital of Kunene Region in the northwestern part of the country. It had a population of 12,000 in 2011.

**Oshikango** is a small town in the northern part of Namibia. It is near the border with Angola. It is also known as a constituency comprising many villages. One of the villages, Okanghudi, is the birthplace of Hifikepunye Pohamba who was president of Namibia from 2005 to 2015. He was the country's second president after Sam Nujoma who led the country to independence from apartheid South Africa.

The town also has many people from Angola who live and trade there.

**Rehoboth** is a town in the central part of Namibia and 56 miles south of Windhoek. There are several natural hot-water springs in the area. In 2005, it had a population of about 29,000 in 2011. Most of the people who live in Rehoboth are Basters. But the Nama people are native to the area.

**Rundu** which is the capital of Kavango-East Region and had a population of about 63,500 in 2011, is the second-largest city in Namibia, after Windhoek, followed by Walvis Bay and Oshakati. Located on the Okavango River, it is also one of the country's commercial centres. It has a "cosmopolitan" outlook and is multilingual.

The city is also known for its shanty towns of Kehemu, Sauyemwa and Ndama; the fourth one, Donkerhoek ( Dark Corner), has become better organised, with fewer informal living quarters.

The country as a whole remains predominantly rural, as most African countries are, in spite of urbanisation in varying degrees.

www.ingramcontent.com/pod-product-compliance
Lightning Source LLC
Chambersburg PA
CBHW051404280526
45784CB00007B/3095